VEGETALES en MiPlato

VEGETABLES on MyPlate

por/by Mari Schuh

Editora consultora/Consulting Editor:
Gail Saunders-Smith, PhD

Consultora/Consultant: Barbara J. Rolls, PhD
Guthrie Chair en Nutrición/Guthrie Chair in Nutrition
Pennsylvania State University
University Park, Pennsylvania

CAPSTONE PRESS
a capstone imprint

Pebble Plus is published by Capstone Press,
1710 Roe Crest Drive, North Mankato, Minnesota 56003
www.capstonepub.com

Library of Congress Cataloging-in-Publication Data
Schuh, Mari C., 1975–
  Vegetales en miplato = Vegetables on myplate / por Mari Schuh ; editora consultora, Gail Saunders-Smith, PhD.
    pages cm. — (Pebble plus bilingüe. ¿Qué hay en miplato? = Pebble plus bilingual. What's on myplate?)
  Spanish and English.
  Audience: K to grade 3
  Includes index.
  ISBN 978-1-62065-948-9 (library binding)
  ISBN 978-1-4765-1766-7 (ebook PDF)
  1. Vegetables—Juvenile literature. 2. Vegetables in human nutrition—Juvenile literature. I. Saunders-Smith, Gail,
editor. II. Schuh, Mari C., 1975– Vegetables on myplate. Spanish. III. Schuh, Mari C., 1975– Vegetables on myplate.
IV. Title. V. Title: Vegetables on myplate. VI. Title: Vegetales en miplato. VII. Title: Vegetables on myplate.
TX557.S38318 2013
641.6'5—dc23   2012022683

Summary: Simple text and photos describe USDA's MyPlate tool and healthy vegetable choices
for children—in both English and Spanish

Editorial Credits
Jeni Wittrock, editor; Strictly Spanish, translation services; Sarah Bennett, designer; Eric Manske, bilingual book
designer; Svetlana Zhurkin, media researcher; Jennifer Walker, production specialist; Sarah Schuette, photo stylist;
Marcy Morin, studio scheduler

Photo Credits
All photos by Capstone Studio/Karon Dubke except:
Shutterstock: Diana Taliun, cover, martascz, back cover; USDA, cover (inset), 5

The author dedicates this book to Rowan Grider of Milwaukee, Wisconsin.

Information in this book supports
the U.S. Department of Agriculture's
MyPlate food guidance system found at
www.choosemyplate.gov. Food amounts
listed in this book are based on daily
recommendations for children ages 4-8.
The amounts listed in this book are
appropriate for children who get less than
30 minutes a day of moderate physical
activity, beyond normal daily activities.
Children who are more physically active
may be able to eat more while staying
within calorie needs. The U.S. Department
of Agriculture (USDA) does not endorse
any products, services, or organizations.

Note to Parents and Teachers

The ¿Qué hay en MiPlato?/What's on MyPlate? series supports national science standards
related to health and nutrition. This book describes and illustrates MyPlate's vegetable
recommendations. The images support early readers in understanding the text. The repetition of
words and phrases helps early readers learn new words. This book also introduces early readers
to subject-specific vocabulary words, which are defined in the Glossary section. Early readers
may need assistance to read some words and to use the Table of Contents, Glossary, Internet
Sites, and Index sections of the book.

Printed in China.
092012   006934LEOS13

Table of Contents

Tabla de contenidos

MyPlate/ MiPlato

Vegetables are a colorful part of MyPlate.
MyPlate is a tool that helps
you eat healthful food.

Los vegetales son una parte colorida de MiPlato.
MiPlato es una herramienta que te
ayuda a comer alimentos saludables.

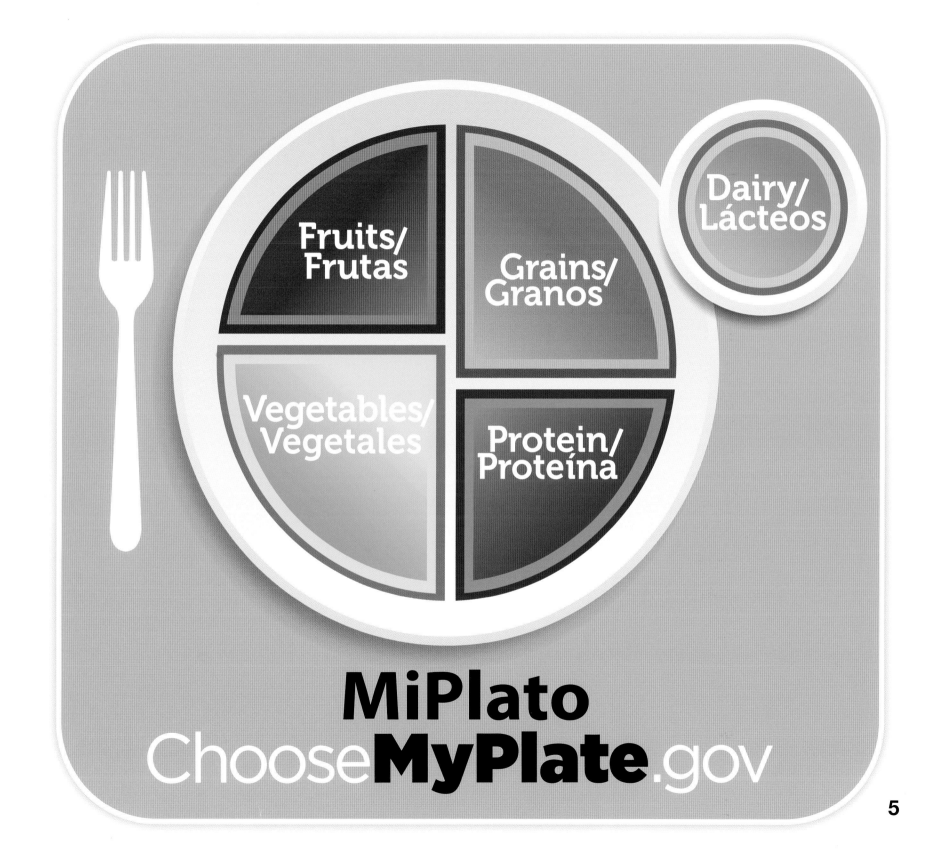

Fruits/
Frutas

Grains/
Granos

Dairy/
Lácteos

Vegetables/
Vegetales

Protein/
Proteína

MiPlato
Choose**MyPlate**.gov

Pass the peas, please!
Fill half your plate
with vegetables and fruit.

¡Pasa los guisantes, por favor!
Llena la mitad de tu plato
con vegetales y fruta.

Each week, eat many
kinds of vegetables.
Every day kids should eat at least
1½ cups (360 milliliters) of vegetables.

Cada semana, come muchos
tipos de vegetales.
Cada día los niños deberían comer por lo
menos 1½ tazas (360 mililitros) de vegetales.

All Kinds of Vegetables/ Todo tipo de vegetales

Vegetables come from plants.
The nutrients in vegetables
keep you healthy and strong.

Los vegetales provienen de plantas.
Los nutrientes en los vegetales te
mantienen saludable y fuerte.

You can enjoy vegetables
in many ways.
Vegetables can be fresh,
canned, frozen, or dried.

Puedes disfrutar los vegetales
de muchas maneras.
Los vegetales pueden ser frescos,
enlatados, congelados o secos.

12

Try different vegetables every day.

Munch on squash, zucchini, and potatoes.

There are so many vegetables
to choose from!

Prueba vegetales diferentes todos los días.

Come zapallo, zucchini y papas.

¡Hay tantos vegetales para seleccionar!

Salads are full of vegetables.

Add cucumbers, carrots, and spinach.

See how many colors you can eat.

Las ensaladas están llenas de vegetales.

Agrega pepinos, zanahorias y espinaca.

Fíjate cuántos colores puedes comer.

Make a veggie pizza
with friends.
Top it with peppers, tomatoes,
and mushrooms.

Prepara una pizza con amigos.
Cúbrela con pimientos,
tomates y champiñones.

How Much to Eat/ Cuánto comer

Kids need to eat at least three servings
of vegetables every day.
To get three servings, pick three
of your favorite vegetables.

Los niños necesitan comer por lo menos tres
porciones de vegetales todos los días.
Para comer tres porciones, selecciona tres
de tus vegetales favoritos.

½ baked potato
½ papa al horno

½ cup (120 mL) broccoli
½ taza (120 ml) de brócoli

½ cup (120 mL) green beans
½ taza (120 ml) de habichuelas verdes

½ cup (120 mL) carrots
½ taza (120 ml) de zanahorias

½ cup (120 mL) split peas
½ taza (120 ml) de guisantes partidos

½ cup (120 mL) tomato juice
½ taza (120 ml) de jugo de tomate

½ cup (120 mL) kidney beans
½ taza (120 ml) de frijoles rojos

½ cup (120 mL) corn
½ taza (120 ml) de maíz

Glossary

MyPlate—a food plan that reminds people to eat healthful food and be active; MyPlate was created by the U.S. Department of Agriculture

nutrient—something that people need to eat to stay healthy and strong; vitamins and minerals are nutrients

serving—one helping of food

vegetable—a part of a plant that people eat; vegetables can be roots, stems, leaves, flowers, or seeds

Internet Sites

FactHound offers a safe, fun way to find Internet sites related to this book. All of the sites on FactHound have been researched by our staff.

Here's all you do:

Visit *www.facthound.com*

Type in this code: 9781620659489

 **Super-cool stuff!** Check out projects, games and lots more at **www.capstonekids.com**

Glosario

MiPlato—un plan de alimentos que hace recordar a la gente de comer alimentos saludables y de estar activos; MiPlato fue creado por el Departamento de Agricultura de EE.UU.

el nutriente—algo que la gente necesita comer para permanecer saludable y fuerte; las vitaminas y los minerales son nutrientes

la porción—una ración de alimento

el vegetal—la parte de una planta que la gente come; los vegetales pueden ser raíces, tallos, hojas, flores o semillas

Sitios de Internet

FactHound brinda una forma segura y divertida de encontrar sitios de Internet relacionados con este libro. Todos los sitios en FactHound han sido investigados por nuestro personal.

Esto es todo lo que tienes que hacer:

Visita *www.facthound.com*

Ingresa este código: 9781620659489

¡Algo súper divertido! Hay proyectos, juegos y mucho más en **www.capstonekids.com**

Index

Índice